Dedicated to my Grandmother— in the case of my gratefulness for you, words could never be enough. I love you, I love you, I love you.

STREAMING

Daniella Rose

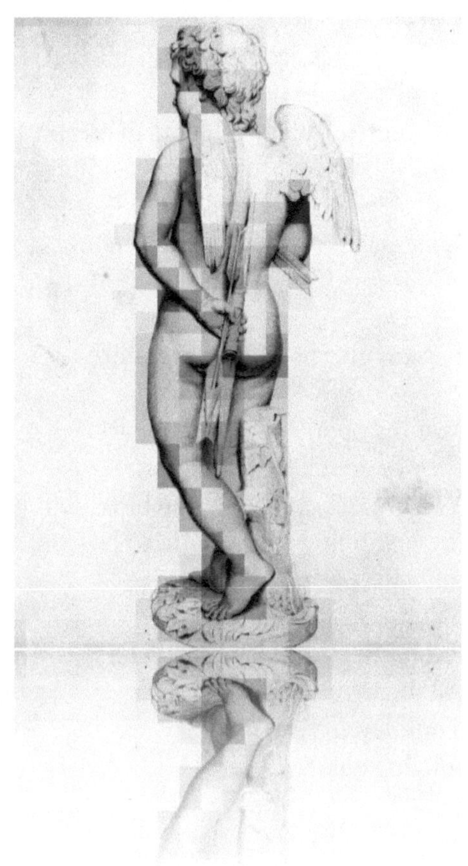

I have not felt your ecstasy before
You are in my visions and I have loved
you always
Everything is covered in prism shards of
divinity
Between us, I am believing in eternity
Can you not tell by earth's shaking
body?
A message from the oracle accounts for
all

Kisses, give oxygen to night fire

Mouths open
From a dream, we were born
You are the crowning, the blossoming,
the beginning–and death, to be itself,
must have life.
Your motion lines the air
Everything is musing over you
All the time
a holiday, a treat
A living elixir

Falling rain, snow, and stars
Merging the forgotten world
Face hot with tears
I was right to fear myself
While I am turning
Into dust thinking
Who will be next?
When I awake
On the other side
Rising up in disbelief
that I made it back to love again

You are my enchantment
I was given my own infinite midnight
Lanterns float in the sky of my mind

Slow burning / hot / bright / lanterns
floating in my mind's sky

These are night activities
Pyramids from the sands of time
Waves crashing stronger than me
Flashes of death
What an unreal scene

Champion lover
Dripping blue
Underworld work
Howling and whipping
Around you like winter wind

Under the onyx blue sea
Sweating in your stone face
My prey
You give me life
Sinking my teeth in
Fire consumes
Mouths open / Silence is a tunnel of
remembering / Eternity is the only /
Uninfluenced of us
It is too late for speech
Night bodies talk in space
Coming to you in your dreams
The fever woke me
In a cold sweat fit
Dream-state gazing
A new sensation
Like pouring, breathing rain
Lightning charging the sky

Each love is begun again
Over and over
We wash the money
We have nothing but this moment
I can see that you know
Gripping cosmic blankets of sky
A slowly written alchemy
Too tender to speak of / Hunting in the
jungle / Hiding in the ocean / Galactic
deserts with ether mirage
What beasts I'm beholding!
These bodies talk in space
Blue lotus chains
floating downriver to paradise

Love pyres carried on the Nile
Paths quiet with hieroglyphs
Onyx bodies in space
An ecstasy virtuoso

An ecstasy in winter
Rogue bliss
Tumbling in white heat
Angel night lights making our faces

Glow like planets suspended in ether
In deep blue obsidian dimensions
Truth captured in a flicker of time
This is your captain speaking
Keep washing the money—

Feeling from ancient depths
Traveling through realms to get to you
In one piece

Line me under the sun
Two more waves in the heat
My eyes drowning extra blue
We don't even have this moment
You and I
Soothed by destruction
Blinded lullaby of other-worlds
Twenty-four karats
Cutting your teeth
Looking at you in danger's rapture
again
I cannot look away from your mystic
movement

walking through you like a portal to
beyond
Birds darting like winged-bullets from
branch to shivering branch
high-rise tree
top paradise
You're a mirage
coming closer to see
if this is real

Cold and heavy, falling
light like snow
falling, collapsing all over myself and
rolling myself out like waves
My heart's song laced with you
like a violin's secret pine
hidden in the echo
of it's every vibration

High heat
high noon
highball
high moon

a violet darkness behind eyelids

again, these numbers show
I am to be satisfied, again
enveloped by loud, deserted night
silence
writhing in my tank beneath red glow

I am the wish
a panther pacing
in onyx shimmer
posing in overnight temperatures

do not be afraid
when a blue light line appears
sparkling at the edge
the muse wants to meet
with you
A flame brushing the shore
testing the wetness of water
how can imperfections exist?
beneath the sun
your bite still
on my throat
what have you done ?

meeting in the snow
te queiro mal
shaking in my shadow
what agony must be endured for just a
peek at ecstasy
you're walking so big
you don't forget we're in the jungle
(lonely and) dizzy with longing
you stand so straight
who is it?
the prey or the prayer?
No one knows
The alchemy of primal comfort
but you, an elixir
for slivers of poison in the mind
(music comes from the muse saying)
"Won't you be my angel today?"
frequency teases friction
things disappear forever
inside eternity

kissed by fire
mars-red cardinal in sight
a drop of blood against the winter snow

...decide how you most like spending
your hours
devouring or being devoured...
Beam through me like sunlight through
sea
blue-black onyx-emerald burning hot
heaven gold (golden heaven) el dorado
blanca fuego white gold a thousand
desert suns gold I turned
To see you looking at me
eyes already clear
dripping colorless
lights flashing through deep water
A sea is never empty
galaxies heavy with stars
lightning splitting
through moody night minds
what can words ever mean ?
Deep blues in deep space
silver, gold, red, chemical emerald
green
we are ornaments adorning
an ancient enchantment
of celestial vines

consuming ourselves
now, each other
A hint of magic is seen
I'm feeling beneath death
Sirens wailing
the sky opens up to us
every second open
even at night
becoming closer, a pearl star
tide coming in
deep waters are here
the rose opens up to us
Venus blossoms swirling
velvet vertigo petals
There are no imperfections under the
sun
the heat on my neck
Riding the dragon lines during wolf's
hour
dominating territory of every blue-black
night

In blood ornamental
veins in midnight blue

How alive do I feel ?
like a mars-fire-red cardinal against the
snow…

Even the odds of indifference
must be in somebody's favor
Riches in the mind
like a panther yawning against a
bejeweled onyx sky…
…bluing like steel
I closed my eyes
this snow is dotting my vision
cast the first stone—

My love, purely political
I am giving you all that you want
because you're going to give me what I
need
Why don't we make prayer ?
we're both on our knees
Won't you be my angel today?
This can be a gateway to Heaven

Quantum-entangled visions of you

bodies going up in steam
onyx leo encircling
God please…
Forgive me
the poison is in my body
intoxicated by youth
feeling so alive, I could die
so far out..
..getting hard to touch down
I need your touch now
Are we free from our vices?
Is freedom our vice ?
Don't let love make you a hypocrite
White sun
Red moon
Hearts beating
fast with purpose
starburst out
of body into
the atmosphere of
the uncontrolled
Every dancing
facet, the destiny
of a blossoming

I reach up to heaven
It's hand reaches down to mine
Heaven walking toward itself
A reflection

Bodies turning over
Sheets shift, a slow twist
Shoulder, then chest, then arm
Rolling like wind-sculpted sands

Storms shaking the city
Black money nights
In the air, I smell your body
lingering spirits

Horses stampeding wild
Waves rising, falling, crashing
A great love,
pharaoh tomb dust
if I think of you
still, even for a second

Words echo in my skull
upon arrival dead

Sapphires, rubies, diamonds
tumbling out of your mouth

My heart is beating so fast
it is breaking so fast
Who is winning this race?
The fissure, shatter, quaking
The breathless dark
The silence of a blow
to the heart

I will be exploded back into a thousand
immortal pieces before I forget your
love

Opals and aquamarine spilling
Lunar ocean, winter moon
…Ice moon, I stagger
Stumbling at glass reflections
Surface illuminated by galaxies
too beautiful to be captured
Do not look at the moon too long
You will stop speaking
All together

Everyone came out once the smoke rose
Under the new moon for you
If I could make love to you tonight
I would never stop
The sound of plucking strings
Cupid burning up
A love so evolved beyond us
We cannot participate as our old selves
A love across time
Once and forever mine
How much power can one pair of eyes
hold?
And when God pulls me to you, why
does it feel so rough?
What doesn't kill you, can still take you
to the edge—
...I love you forever
I love you always
I love you beyond
I love you all days
Every lover has been my favorite
Every person has been my love
Let it be here on earth
As it is so above

This poem is a record of a trance that I have been in all the time, while I am doing everything else, this is going on in the background of my psyche.   There are repeated words, fragmented phrases, inconsistent punctuation, along with randomizing the use of capital lettering. This was done deliberately and meant to express a hypnotic, stream-of-consciousness-styled articulation.   Love, in all its forms, was the genesis of the subconscious impassioned state which birthed these words. Always running in my unconscious mind even, love is humming unceasingly.   I consider this to be a love poem, but love does not always have a romantic connotation.

Love can make life heavy or light, it can fuel impenetrable allegiance, create angst and war, it can breathe life into deadness.   But sometimes there are things love teaches us which have nothing to do with love itself, and in that way, this poem is about whatever it felt like to you. Thank you for reading and no matter what happens, remain *in love*.